THE STORY OF CHRISTMAS

Edited by Solveig Muus

TABLE OF CONTENTS

ISBN 978-1-936020-30-0

Imagine Life Without Christmas

Imagine Bethlehem the day before Jesus was born.

The next day would not be Christmas, because the beautiful baby we know as the Son of God wasn't in the manger yet.

No choirs were singing "Peace on earth" or "Good will to all" or any other Christmas song. No Christmas trees.

People were lonesome in those days. They said to each other, "I wonder if God really loves us?" They wished that God did not seem so far away.

This made God sad. It made people sad, too, because no matter what they did, they could never be good enough for a Pure, Holy, and Perfect God.

But all hope was not lost, because God had a plan.

CHRISTMAS PRAYER

O Lord, long ago You promised to send us a
Redeemer born of a virgin.
When You were ready, You sent us Your Son, Jesus,
born of the Virgin Mary. Please help us prepare the way for
Jesus to be born again in our hearts this Christmas. Amen.

The Prophecies

God created Adam and Eve to know, love, and serve Him on earth and be happy with Him forever in heaven. When Adam and Eve disobeyed God and lost heaven, God promised to send them a redeemer.

Through the years, God sent prophets to tell His people about this redeemer, the Messiah. Their messages were called prophecies. Jesus fulfilled every prophecy made about Him!

One of the greatest prophets, Isaiah, said that the Messiah would be born of a virgin, and he would be called Immanuel, which means "God with us." The virgin was Mary, and Jesus was her Son. Micah the prophet announced that the Messiah would be born in Bethlehem, which is the town where Jesus was born.

John the Baptist was the cousin of Jesus, and he helped people get ready to accept Jesus as their Messiah.

"Therefore the Lord himself will give you this sign: the virgin shall be with child, and bear a son, and shall name him Immanuel."
ISAIAH 7:14

The Annunciation

God chose certain people to do a particular work for Him. The most special of these was Mary, a virgin who lived in a little town in Israel called Nazareth.

One day an angel named Gabriel appeared to Mary and said, "Hail Mary! You are full of grace. Do not be afraid, for the Lord is with you!" Gabriel told Mary that God wanted her to bear His Son, and to call His name Jesus. Mary said, "Behold, I am the handmaid of the Lord. May it be done unto me as you have said."

Mary obeyed God. Because she said yes, Jesus was born, God was able to save the world, and the gates of heaven were opened.

Mary is our model, and also our mother. We should always ask her help to obey God and to be like Jesus. If we follow Mary, she will lead us to her Son.

"And coming to her, he said, 'Hail, favored one!
The Lord is with you. ... Do not be afraid, Mary, for you have
found favor with God. Behold, you will conceive and bear a son,
and you shall call him Jesus.'"
LUKE 1:28, 30-31

Mary Visits Elizabeth

When Mary awoke the next morning, she felt happy. The angel's message to her seemed almost too good to be true.

Mary remembered that the angel had told her that her cousin, Elizabeth, was also expecting a child. Mary decided to visit her.

Mary got dressed, ate, and let her family know where she was going. Then she set off on a journey to Judea where her cousin lived.

It took Mary a few days, so when she arrived at the home of Zacharias and Elizabeth, she was very weary from the long journey.

Elizabeth hurried to share the good news with Mary about what the Lord had done, but as soon as she saw Mary and heard her voice, the baby inside her jumped with joy!

At that moment, Elizabeth was filled with the Holy Spirit. She cried, "Blessed are you among women, and blessed is the baby you carry! It is such a blessing that you came to visit me, the mother of my Lord."

"When Elizabeth heard Mary's greeting, the infant leaped in her womb, and Elizabeth, filled with the holy Spirit, cried out, 'Most blessed are you among women, and blessed is the fruit of your womb!'"
LUKE 1:41-42

The Journey to Bethlehem

Meanwhile, back in Nazareth, an angel of the Lord came to Joseph in a dream. The angel said, "I have come to tell you that Mary, your betrothed, will have a son sent by God. You will name him Jesus. He will save his people from their sins." After Joseph heard this, he married Mary and cared for her tenderly.

Not long after Joseph and Mary were married, the Roman emperor, Caesar Augustus, decreed that all people should pay taxes. But first, everyone had to go back to his birthplace to have his name written on a list.

Joseph and Mary needed to have their names written on Caesar's list too. Joseph was of the family of King David, whose birthplace was Bethlehem. So from Nazareth they traveled down the mountains to the river Jordan. They followed the long river almost to its end. Then they climbed up the mountains of Judah, until, finally, they reached the little town of Bethlehem.

"In those days a decree went out from Emperor Augustus
that all the world should be registered.
All went to their own towns to be registered."
LUKE 2:1, 3

No Room at the Inn

The stars shone dimly that night in Bethlehem as Joseph and Mary searched for a place to rest. The town bustled with people who had come to have their names written on the emperor's list. No one knew that Mary was about to give birth to the Son of God. Everywhere they went, people said, "There is no room for you."

Mary paused to feel the cool wind on her face and the ache in her weary bones. She knew that her time had come. She would give birth that very night.

Joseph tried again to find a place for Mary to rest. He found a small inn and knocked at the door. When a man answered the door, Joseph asked, "Do you have a room where we can sleep tonight?"

"I'm sorry," the man said. "My inn is full. There is no room for you here."

"Joseph also went from the town of Nazareth in Galilee to Judea, to the city of David called Bethlehem, because he was descended from the house and family of David. He went to be registered with Mary, to whom he was engaged and who was expecting a child."
LUKE 2:4-5

Jesus Is Born

Then the man at the inn looked at Mary's face. He could see how much she needed a place to rest. "You can sleep in the stable with the animals," he said. "It is the best I can do for you."

They went to the stable where Mary could rest, surrounded by the comforting sounds of the farm animals. Joseph made a bed for her out of the softest hay he could find.

There, in the stable in Bethlehem, Mary gave birth to the baby Jesus. She wrapped him in swaddling clothes to keep him warm. Joseph found a manger being used to feed the cows and oxen. He used it to make a tiny bed for the baby. Mary laid her little baby in the manger and watched over him as he slept.

"And she gave birth to her firstborn son and wrapped him
in bands of cloth, and laid him in a manger,
because there was no place for them at the inn."
LUKE 2:7

The Shepherds in the Field

That night, under the same starry sky, some shepherds tended their flocks of sheep in a nearby field.

Suddenly the sky exploded with light, frightening the poor shepherds. Out of the light, an angel of the Lord appeared to them and said,

"Do not be afraid, for I bring you good tidings of great joy for all people. This day in Bethlehem a Savior is born who is Christ the Lord. You will find him wrapped in swaddling cloths, lying in a manger."

A great gathering of angels joined the first angel. Together they sang their praises to God. "Glory to God in the highest," they sang. "And on earth, peace, good will toward men."

"Then an angel of the Lord stood before them, and the glory
of the Lord shone around them, and they were terrified.
But the angel said to them, 'Do not be afraid; for see – I am
bringing you good news of great joy for all the people: to you is born
this day in the city of David a Savior, who is the Christ, the Lord.'"
LUKE 2:9-11

The Shepherds Rejoice

The shepherds looked at each other in awe. Was it true that the Savior had come at last and so near to their own humble homes? "Let us hurry," the shepherds said to one another. "Let us go now to Bethlehem."

The shepherds found Joseph and Mary in the stable watching over the baby asleep in the manger. "We were in the field," they said to Mary and Joseph, "and an angel came and told us the news."

The next day, the shepherds told the people in the village all the things the angel had said. Their story amazed everyone who heard it. Mary smiled at these things with wonder and kept them quietly in her heart.

The shepherds returned to their field praising God for all they had seen and heard.

"The shepherds said to one another, 'Let us go now to Bethlehem and see this thing that has taken place, which the Lord has made known to us.' So they went in haste and found Mary and Joseph, and the child lying in the manger."
LUKE 2:15-16

The Journey of the Magi

Some time after Jesus was born, wise men called Magi also came to visit him. They had traveled a long way on camels and horses to the land of Judea.

Bethlehem was in Judea, but at first the Magi went to Jerusalem. They asked everyone, "Where is he who has been born King of the Jews? For we have seen his star in the East and have come to worship him." But no one seemed to know.

King Herod, the old ruler of Judea under Caesar, was jealous and afraid. He demanded that the chief priests of the people tell him where to find this baby. "In Bethlehem," they told him.

King Herod sent the Magi to Bethlehem to search for the baby. "If you find him," King Herod said, "let me know, so I can go and worship him too." But secretly, old King Herod had an evil plan to kill the baby.

"Wise men from the East came to Jerusalem, asking,
'Where is the child who has been born king of the Jews? For we
observed his star at its rising, and have come to pay him homage.'"
MATTHEW 2:1-2

The Gifts of the Magi

The Magi continued on their journey. At night, they looked up to find the same bright star they had followed before. They happily followed it again, this time all the way to Bethlehem. There the star came to shine over the baby Jesus.

The Magi saw the baby with his mother, Mary, and knew at once that he was the king. They fell down on their knees and worshiped him as the Lord. Then they opened their treasures and gave him gifts of gold, frankincense, and myrrh.

That night, God warned the Magi in a dream not to go back and tell King Herod about the baby Jesus. So they went back home a different way.

God also sent a warning to Joseph. Joseph secretly took Mary and the baby Jesus away to hide in Egypt. There they safely stayed as long as the evil King Herod lived.

"On entering the house, they saw the child with Mary his mother; and they knelt down and paid him homage. Then, opening their treasure chests, they offered him gifts of gold, frankincense and myrrh."
MATTHEW 2:11

The Flight into Egypt

This is how God sent a warning to Joseph. An angel of the Lord appeared to him and said, "Take your wife and young child and flee to Egypt, and remain there until I tell you to come back. Herod is going to search for the child to destroy him."

Because of his strong faith, Joseph knew that the angel came from God, and he trusted what the angel said. So late that night, Joseph took his wife and Jesus and the donkey and they made the long journey to Egypt.

After two years the Lord told Joseph, "Don't worry anymore, King Herod is dead! You can return home to Nazareth now."

Joseph packed up the little donkey and brought Mary and Jesus back to Nazareth. Joseph and Mary loved and cared for Jesus, who seemed to grow more loving and wise every year. When Mary looked at Jesus, she thought about his birth. In her heart, she thanked God for her son. Someday the whole world would know of Jesus, but for now, he was just her little boy.

MATTHEW 2:14-15

Christmas Tree Blessing

Dear God our Father,

Holy Creator of Trees and of all living things,

bless with Your abundant grace

this our Christmas tree as a symbol of joy.

May its evergreen branches be a sign

of Your never-fading promises.

May its colorful lights and ornaments call us

to decorate with love our home and our world.

May the gifts that surround this tree

be symbols of the gifts we have received

from the Tree of Christ's Cross.

Holy Christmas tree within our home,

may Joy and Peace come and nest

in your branches and in our hearts. Amen.

Christmas Gift Prayer

Thank you, God for the wonderful gift of Your Son, Jesus, as we celebrate His birthday. Help us to remember Him as we give and receive gifts, taking time to pray for each person and for those who have nothing. Help us, Lord, to fill this Christmas with You and with Your love, peace, and joy. Amen.

Christmas Eve Prayer

Loving God, help us remember the birth of Jesus, that we may share in the song of the angels, the gladness of the shepherds, and the worship of the wise men.

Close the door of hate and open the door of love all over the world. Let kindness come with every gift and good desires with every greeting. Deliver us from evil by the blessing which Christ brings, and teach us to be merry with clear hearts.

May Christmas morning make us happy to be Thy children, and Christmas evening bring us to our beds with grateful thoughts, forgiving and forgiven, for Jesus' sake. Amen.

~Robert Louis Stevenson

A Prayer for Christmas Eve

This is the most special night of year, the night of our dear Savior's birth! Advent has come to an end, and now it is time to celebrate the great and wonderful feast of Christmas!

Let us pray together:

Dear God, thank You for bringing us through the Advent season to this holy night. May our hearts be ever open to receive You and to receive others in Your name. Help us celebrate with great joy the birth of Your Son, Our Lord Jesus Christ.

Help us to bring Your Christmas joy, love, and peace to all people. Help us to be more kind to one another, more patient, and more forgiving. Please bless Your world with peace, and fill us with Your Spirit this blessed night. In Jesus' name. Amen.